HOW TO ORDER EGGS SUNNY SIDE UP

Lisa Collyer

HOW TO ORDER EGGS SUNNY SIDE UP

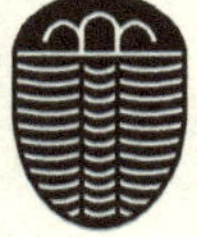

WOMEN SQUEEZE MY BREASTS TO CHECK HOW MUCH TIME IS LEFT ...

How to Order Eggs Sunny Side Up

I am Alice's diary. She is my neighbour, so we talk open-air over a closed book. We live on Christmas Island, a limestone seamount terraced by an indentured past. Alice is Chinese-Malay, I am European—together we perform *wayang kulit* (a shadow play) of cultural harmony. We celebrate festivities in turn; so I take oranges to Chinese homes, suns of gold—the right number are pairs but never four. I have olive skin-tan like hers, but she is bullied by female kin who stay indoors. At thirty-four, I try to conceive but each month an egg cooks defective. I wish I had Alice while touring Malaysia to help me order eggs sunny side up. The first question I'm asked is whether I have children. I learn to say, *belum* (not yet) for the truth is unpalatable. Women squeeze my breasts to check how much time is left—they are round like apples in pairs, but not sun gold like oranges. I want to order eggs sunny side up, but I only know *rebus* (boiled), hard and grey not soft and gooey and *kuning* (yellow) whisked 'til cracked. I am *orang putih* (white) even though I'm tan hide, and my boyfriend's hands are third degree burnt. People whisper, *bakar* (baked). When I cycle Vietnam, my skin leathers, hard cracked under the sun's knell, but the only sunscreen I can find is whitening. I don't want to be light, nor do I want to be baked, so I shadow puppet like a local woman, a silhouette behind white drape. It takes three days to order eggs sunny side up. I draw a gold sun setting on an island of colour blind. The cook pinpoints the words, *mata sapi*. I taste them individually, in turn. Eye. Cow. Bull's eye.

MAIDEN SHAME

Before a nymph learns to gag
I sieve the letters you explete
bilious   S   L
U
T   like you know
delinquent fingers
give pudency the slip
prise the cache to peak
threefold.
It's only the summit
but one stands taller than the rest.
A bundle of *sticks*
clenched *and stones* thrown.

Needlework

It's hard to believe
the butterfly fruit service is pristine.

Her hair parts—split peel.
The candlelight projects a crowning calyx.

The double bed's iron legs—
a pedestal of balaustine fruit.

The crewel stitch of an intricate knot
to mend scored pith.

A slap to revive
a delicate constitution.

A pomegranate rupture
on hairpin lace.

Bildungsroman

There are two hundred and eighty-three steps
between *childhood*
and *home*, a rite to an uncertain future.
I try to delay the advent
idle heel-to-toe, leave no gaps.
My left heel strikes the ground
between my best friend's house
and a knife hurtled.
The footpath absorbs the scream
my left arch rears
the keystone bears the load.
A schoolgirl's scoliosis forms a question mark
and asks, *why me?*
But a time lapsed gait still journeys to a destination.
I fail to disembark heart from mouth
dissociate at traitor's gate
tripped by guilt.
Each foot rolled like my adolescence.

1 IN 4

If I were to uncoil
lower tongue
and exhale
my unmarked teeth
could serve a family epitaph—
a tabloid typeface
smudged Franklin Gothic
no gun buyback
would redress.

IN SICKNESS

Slip beneath the sheet
I hurt for touch
a carer-cum-spouse
your reach is task based
shy away from pitiful romance
teeth brushed too hurriedly
bemoan the gums
the probing tongue
the kiss of life
bristles.
Your aspirations shoehorn
a chin's ploy
to waylay time
into hospital corners
allotted to my care
the sheets susurrate
a towelette graze
dependable intimacy
is three-day tuft
as you begrudge each stitch
remembrance of caresses.
You wear guilt lace tied off
to prevent bleed out.
Your breath snags (I see)

you're expected to smile
when the gauze grazes
you wipe away my piss
your sex
lust lost to catheters rent
shame is catalyst—
urine-soaked tracksuit pants.
Bodies touched are seen.
You gag. *I anticipate. Chastise*
rush to part my lips
crack the closet
an impediment to swallow.
Climb the family tree
the water bites
die a little death
in a shower made for two
map the warp
and the weft
implore polygynous hands
to loiter.
A nightcap restraint
I beseech your dispensation
hitch the road out.
Stay a little longer.

THE BEAUTY POLICE

I strip
search for woman
but there is only girl. A constant
vigil of unwanted hair for removal.

I tame
fur lined lips tied to Mediterranean
roots—threatening to unravel
a farce constructed to fit.

I betray
flesh razed in wax strips
fleecing skin & hard-won purse
—a depilation identikit.

I detangle self from family
trussed to tresses. A domination
of foreign threads.

The aesthetic dictates a glabrous lip
centrefold—in a denuded line-up
under duress.

Mother I'd Like to ...

after Breakfast at Tiffany's

F. baby, you should've kept
the sweet shop, a walk-in-robe
holiday leave with your squeeze
a typewriter ribbon's loose knot
an independent MILF
you'll adore the upholstered
wingback—screw up the waif's
promissory, seal off the fire
escape, you need your sleep
you've got booty call on rotary dial
bucks to visit the gent's
you could've written a popular novel
by now, film acquisitions to boot
instead, you shacked up with a flake
a real baloney.

IMPOSSIBLE JEANS

after Denim Day

It creeps. Rifles her body—absolves blame
nodding assent to her undoing. In jeans
solidarity surrounds wounded fruit
hounds' bare teeth outraged by unjust decree.
A protest captures wind change in ancient
piazza. A limpet undone, traction
lost to wayward nerve. They all wear jeans
disrupting parliament, dissidents bay
in protest of the judge's verdict—that
it's impossible to rape a woman
wearing jeans. It annihilates. Raided
fabric plunders breaching boundaries of
what little flesh. It insinuates. Frayed
breaths whisper—a culprit of poor choices.
Her body is sacked, Rome is in ruins
legitimising lawlessness. Undone.
She bears slander—bequeathed shame.
Cheeks turn raw and razed. He flees pardoned.
She seeks asylum—back against sullied walls
to lean. Uneven bird shit drips, stains stone
paths piercing soles of unsupportive flimsy
sandals. Judgemental leer points, penetrates
resolve. The bench marks her jeans. Undone.
Even in jeans.

Reagent

Before this photograph
    I can be seen running
    through light to successive
        dark room liaisons
too impatient to develop
attachment.

But by way of a Kahlua
    promotion, we have a polaroid
    of our first date. The film pants
        expectant of a chemical
attraction, thighs lead-in a hair's
breadth split.

The press of a shutter-release
    the colour spectrum of luculent
    flesh, wide open to exposure.
        To earth sparks
outrun time, snap backs
against walls

framed to foretell—
he is the last.

Baby on Board

It was no contest
to be the first
to lay down
traction
in the passenger
seat
a dry mouth
drags
on the clutch
of a sphincter
bulls stamp
a red light
white knuckled smoke

mash a burnt palate
a charge
in a cranial cradle
burnt out
fuel exhausted
the tinkle
of laughter.

A Triptych

1.
There's no need to peep
I am public space
demurely rendered.
Catch a glimpse—
a nude in a tub trope,
not impressions of light
but utility as scullery maid
to wash and churn butter
pats, calloused hands—toast
to her tiptop white.

2.
Get down
from your landing of lofty
pursuit to ground toilette in pastel
mundanity. Be useful and scrub my back.

3.
I am the water bearer
my basin is brimful.
I master brush and comb
accoutrements of rank
but today I see through vanity
and mock glass;
a coquettish glance in the wings
at a fine deportment
work worn and ripped.

Dishonour

he came ooh-ing and aah-ing
fiddling his doorknob
thighs glad, drunk, broke

evil fleece, stay home
some mistake
a nightmare
a dumb box

why are girls here?
keep in their rooms, a body
a crime, bold girl
to dare exist

her blood like some natural dignity
a grave, another dick
choked and loved

a woman's behaviour is wrong
he was just honest
women want
to give sex

she said, I was beaten
the problem was
the legs, the ass
downstairs to snack on

I Have Two Pregnancy Stories

you tell me yours and I'll keep mum

one
am I dying?
the gym circuit follows
punitive foetal curl ups
I shred guts
in the same bed
blankets in shambles
now sluice
an Egyptian screw
into the bog

two
        no need to check
a knowing
breasts spill, waistband
kick backs
follows
        ink on slip
unknowing, it's illegal
        then
on my back, he comes too
        yes, it's what I want
the lights instruct
        put your bottom down, miss
follows
sucking it all

Brittle

If I could take back—I would
scrape tongue of bitter words
that blister heart on impact.

Take acrid words—spit them back
burn lips & make them seep
a caustic, gore drip.

It's not true what I said
save that I said it.
Spite told, I love you
for mere want of want to hurt.

I am inept at most things
except hurt, hurt I get fat on.
If I could wash out acid pit
—I would.

Shatterproof

after Amélie

What if I were glass?
my bones fired sand
fragility blown-out
coddle my delicate glaze

What if I declare, I can't cope?
send the grocery boy up
with foie gras and artichoke
in bechamel sauce

… to teach him vitriol
What if I am the man
of glass dependant on the girl
upstairs to set the time?

THE LADETTE

after the silver nutmeg grater bearing the initials J.S.R (John Septimus Roe)

Into the punch, her rebellion is rum.
A nutmeg pinch over a boundary
feud. An earring lost is tiddly peach
blossom, the flood levels the fence
line, a moveable feast of insect swarm.
She wangles personal stakes, ottomans
the ringtone of tin pannikins, a slutty
citrus cleaves to a punchbowl attired to
stir-up broken tea. She tries not to rouse
the surveyor, missteps into a stiletto
slips over a bra strap. Plot lines survey
her midriff as she scrabbles for bounty
and panties, still punch drunk she falls flat
on a pillow, a holy shroud of mascara and
rouge. The room rasps—post-divorce reflux.

Just Looking

after 'Window Shopping at The Taxidermist's' *by John Kinsella*

A wire twist—shoulder-like—hangs
blonde ambition, more elastic than
a syncopated rhythm. A lick of silk,
the lace rasp of tongue and as a lining
a teddy rides-up with a proclivity to lodge
camel toe. The flapper is loose, breasts are
strapped down, all heads turn on a collar-
bone slope. Are you wanting to play
like a flamboyance of pink? The intent
is to browse, the ironed skin, the coif,
the silhouette. Here, they flaunt their wares,
click bait to consume not a stitch.

Abnormal Beauty

after 'Children are the Orgasm of the World' *by Hera Lindsay Bird*

At 9:05, I enter the Myer City department store and there is a banner with a slogan attached to a product name, I've already forgotten, *your gift, their difference.* I like products that remind me, as a woman if I do something for myself, it should benefit others. The bullet-belt of lipsticks for all mouths. all shades. all currency. attracts me to its potency. I trace my finger along the scar on a male model reclining at the top of an escalator always going the wrong way. The decompression zone offers a *slow hand* and a colour swatch match to *Marrakesh intense* and I just know I'm what they call *spicy*. I'm drawn to the *abnormal beauty* catchphrase finding it familiar, but I'm distracted by a Socratic line of questioning. What is abnormal beauty? And can you provide an example? I look around and the only one I find is a model with a diastema and it reminds me that I had a gap in my front teeth once, but a dentist filled it in without asking. The product displays of handbags are in odd numbers, and I think about the consequences of assuming and observe that the abnormal range sat further back from the central display.

Italicised words are from marketing slogans.

THE HAIR SALON

I enter the hall of mirrors: an illusion
of choice, amazed at the promise of spoils
women crowned in tin foil. The air shrieks
a solution of bleach, miscalculate measures
of colour for youth. Briny almanacs record
trials to preserve: a labyrinth of time lost
to the untenable. I scry my womanhood
a divine silver lineage through cracked
glass, dead end and blackened. The stylist's
shears fit to spay, fast lipped and metallic
snip and erase, swept away by the inevitable
broom. I appear silvern, fade to brave when
a pretty girl slips into the pyre. Fate cackles:
takes my money but does not see me leave.

Argent Cast

Silver foil—the glitterati of
middle age, no need to shy
from adoration. Let them
throw roses at your feet,
you who've hidden, filigree
of inhibition—a backdrop behind
red drape. It's time to undress
Mercutio.

IBS

after 'to Nannup' *by Kevin Gillam*

I incur physiological angst.
I inherit
abdominal scream.

I incur
memories of meals ate
which don't distend. I inherit

vapours that inflate a cleaved gut
—the pain it is. I inherit fodmaps,
plan meals around them

then mis-recollect. I inhabit
fidgets in navigating dishes
to choose. I inherit

flush days of intestinal health
until irritability follows. I incur
plain tastes, pre-empt chickpeas

in vegetable stew. I inhabit
wail
foodies howl to wind. I inherit

an undiagnosable palate as they
rollick in phosphates as I cuss. I incur
fastidious habits

dispiriting pride. I inherit
a fear of cream and cabbage—
antagonising muck. I inherit
infinite recipes for
windless plates. I incur
depressing inexplicable

symptoms that cripple days. I inherit
a groomed plan—loose skirt—unseen
but never to me. I inherit
pain
resist grimace. I inhabit
pain.

I inherit a toxic gut. I incur
physiological angst.

THE PENCIL TEST

Liberty is a bare breast. The pencil test
is a woman's measure—H for hard.
A stylus marks the inframammary crease
to support the sacred cup. Some *ptsosis*,
naturally, they are no longer parallel
to the clavicle, but the aureoles still halo
pincellus. A technician scoops a *champagne*
coupe to crush between teeth. A deficit
of maternal is opaquely dense breasts.
Saint Agatha's trial deciphers if she's
diseased. Her face, a Berlei pink to snap
straps. She sits blue in a hospital gown,
a questionnaire collates her metre from one
to ten, being fret on repeat with each new
pinch. Liberty is a bare breast. The lubed prod
of a sonographer's pitch in a freedom trash can.
A spring-loaded prick takes a bite. Pussy Riot
invites Mary to renege the demands on her milk.
The same pencil that measured her height
each birthday.

Thanatosis

Cease Keres! I am asbestos in exile
playing possum. A cot-queen
of bedsore retardant, a pressed posey
of floorboard damp. I desist
your nightjar gale, your wet flame
of louvred breath to billow the jib.
I pin the bedsheets to a dormitory
hulk and sip cocktails from a muslin-
capped tea-service to muzzle the sound
of brux.

... AND I EVOLVE TEETH.

Floral Bodies

A possum-like inflorescence
gestates beneath gums
cream, gold, and brown
I tangle fingers in woolly hairs
belly, bottom, ears, and mouth
like lanugo in utero.

I count your parts
like Ferdinand Bauer's
Banksia illustrations
anatomically correct
floral head, stems, and bracts
fingers and toes.

Seasonally, I imagine
I trod a different path
I follow the natal trajectory
of Artemis' arrow and I keep you
intact.

A whimsical thought
of feminine birth
I bury our placental bond
(the interface of our intimacy)
swaddled in Teatree infused bark.

But I return to accuracy
when the blunt point pierces
my womb—
a wooden cone
whose nut stops growing
my body burns
a follicle bursts
and you evacuate
unable to handle
crisis.

And I evolve teeth.

For Display Purposes Only

A pearl shell deflects a grand theft
to show visitors and a Jarrah is brought
down to size by a two-man crosscut.
We preserve a shelled walnut to archive
the price paid for a flesh wound.
The dining room is genteel in situ
cordoned-off to safeguard the past.
A knife box is a mahogany urn, its secrets
are conversation starters. Postcode snobs
gossip on tree-lined streets and capital gains
glint on each tine. A diorama is shelved
to outlast the gums of banked habitat.
The eucalypt sheds sentiment but the children
eschew the barricade tape and straddle its girth.

Soft Country, Hard Hooves

Far from cities of art patents
on Parade Cows—pageant or pin-up
we journey to that place
outback
to pick at bones.

We cleave city from bush
down a knife-pleat runway
a Spring revue of supine stock
point cloven heels
to Dark Emu.

We curate the mythology of us
calibrate lens on the prettiest pouts
a wreath appliques the verge
a death mask
floral emblem.

A cattle-call card to calculate
kill weight—meat charts
sirloin, shoulder, or brisket
roadkill is not having time
to bury the dead.

Inflated they waft
unlike city-slick bovine—in peplum
boarding a train—herd
clicking their heels
down Main St.

We dry retch at a flyblown ribcage
the empire waist of winnowing topsoil
compacts to dust
a diorama of obsolete
stitched skin.

We pass signs of stray animals
that impede progress, a kangaroo paw
clutches sovereignty
from a fur stole carcass
in a roadhouse carpark.

We proclaim allegiance
to not eat our crest
spite soft country, hard hooves
we insist on beef: live strut
or boxed on ice.

We stride, stomp back, scrape
the highway for bull bar jerky
a post-apocalyptic Spring
shades the wide-open space.

Ruth's Reproach

after Jasper Jones *by Craig Silvey*

I need parted lips and real holes filled
but you peak on narrative climax. Lipstick
smeared wino's kiss, barefoot and punk
on the backseat of the family car. I fumble
with bleach over grass stains and goop glued
to a see-through dress. My peach nail veneer
is chipped yet still you insist the maid is quiet.
I power serve a backhand cup of instant spite
my last card to escape your limp impotence—
a trick-take on the town's skirt. Best you dig
the hole from whence you foaled and return
to the horse's uterus.

Offal Intimacy

Saturday morning treat—
Brylcreem in sideburns
dissolved salt scum
porcine and honeycomb tripe.
I hover to get close
but he keeps me in the flanks
I'm not your boyfriend.
Pig's trotters. I stomach sticky
tendons, wayward stubble
incises, tongue to jimmy out
the gristle between toes.
The seventies orange tablecloth
elbows take-off—
etiquette is hands-on
blood lines in jelly.
I try to get close.

Ramp of Resignation

It was the last chance to be handled
by a man, rubbed-up against a stiff
in the gentleman's change room.
Many of us succumbed to unlatched
ennui, there was no sense you were
leaving any other way. A halfway hitch
between doors, a wind gap whistling.

State of Emergency

Do closed eyes see the light?
I bargain with a sunbeam deity
to save him—
a Lenten sacrifice.
Tubes invigilate eternal flame
bellow oxygen into every orifice
the relief of a cerebral swell
a tinderbox front in the Adelaide Hills
a spot fire siren, the topography
of violet.
Ash rains to mark us
flags half-mast—a public crisis
our private pain
where the only grace is sunset.

Carnal Rites

to eat flesh
prepare to kill
the lamb's embrace
more a crack than a break

I take the knife, a swift slit
an oblatory slump
sorry

what happens next?
a hanging—the hook bleeds
the trough catches
damn spot

he photographs exsanguination
careful slits, arse up
pulls down skin like pants

what about the meat?
two fingers insert—nick tissue
viscera spills, a warm body

in bed, lovers bleat
It's what I want

Waxen Limbs

My body in segments   I part
a wild creature, finger nap

loose strands catch
in wax seal. I paddle

sweet hiss, wrestle
stiction, prime and slather

limbs in burnt
drool, delirious heat. I pick

where wingbeats pulse: nexus
of sting

a hive shivers
last seen
at the shin

hot
against me
one last tug

here on the cool tiles.

A Rare Bird

On a paddleboard I stand
on a body of water.
Feet plant parallel
to the embank- ment
and I look outward
and try to recall the names of birds.
I feather my blade efficiently
incompressible resistance
propels me forth.
The fin trails aquatic weed
a lure to snag but I can't conjure
swan today tho' I bugle
swan song in two tongues.
A ribbon grant unfurls
a street sign namesake
whence shot swan lain limp.
The neck is a river bend.
I stand perpendicular
to that body.

Mine

Gold dowry splits
lobes. I am disfigured
by the weight of gold.
A scar trucks
on an open pit
across my pubis.
They extract a girl
a gift of gold
supposed to be mine.
We bury her blue
—cover in sand
grain-sized pieces.
I want to drown
in a cyanide mouthwash
around gold crowns
but I wear black.

Flyway

I stand apart   a drab donga. Zipped vests undo
basic plumage, almost
    non-verbal. Rare vagrant, ropy
lists.   In the shadehouse, species queue
into rows and
    columns. Rivals split over a ka ke
ki-ki-ki. I acculturate an ornithological gait, my next
meal, my next
    mate. Spotting scopes   strewn over fold-out
tables,   outdo sweaty prints on digital stills
(apertures of truth) not yet showered.
    They are all ecru, each unidentifiable.
A migrant's prosody draws a mob
to ogle
    lurid eye-stripe. Squadrons form orderly
whilst I lag like the return flight.
A bat hangs
    atrophied.
How I have changed? Peripatetic
follower of quiet observation.   I sit out
    the doldrums in a peep   hole. One Bower-
bird—hoard theory verified. Blind stoics, two
Peaceful Doves, and a mantle of delineated
    bars. I settle for unspoilt real estate
a prayer of Godwits on a midden's scatter.

Myth Management

The Wedge-tail turns dragon slayer
in an attraction of prescribed fury
one vanishing act at a time.
The Powder Bark sheds dust
—a shallow gallery of urns, stick
incense flickering out. Fanned breath
down a hot collar, a litter in defeat.
Are there hollows left?
No pouch to turn into a lignotuber's
hide, an animal emblem raised on a lapel
is mythic. Return fire to sender,
it's squandered in our hands, triage
conservation ministers a tongue licking flare
on the Red List.

Plastic Sleeve

The reinforced spine
fused vertebrae
cartilaginous flim-flam
ice cores punched to dispose.
We buy them in packs of one-
hundred to contain late nights
before school begins
curriculum links in tables
authentic learning colour coded
Times New Roman.
Real life. We can't wear them
raglan cut, armpit to neckline
we teach one size fits all
relevant education.
Aspire to self-worth.
Bottle-up ice floes.
Cradle a life examined
reuse and recycle. On muck-up
day their shoulders emancipate
upright spines in plastic moulds.
Authentic learning
first thing binned.

TO THE SEA

We face down
the Anthropocene
sieve breath
through plastic
fragments of death
(a talisman to Thalassa)
ghost-like
around our necks.
Trace fish, fabled gills
sunlit pins
and purple flags
we long to hold onto
            your carapace
ascend   to share breath
and escape
a sea burial.
Relinquish spine
transcend coral, trembling lace
ransacked of blush, bone
to dust
a triggerfish listing
            sinks
in the last
light.   A surge hiss
lures us
into the maelstrom
a sea of teeth
we are the eye
regress to Chaos—
loosen
plastic bit.

Biota

There's refuge in what wetland's left. A plastic bag seals-off the windpipe
of a jointed rush, upbeat paperbarks extend, others exfoliate and lean-to.

I navigate the winter solstice like a faded slogan. The arboretum's desire
line, no left turn at the chinked chain for dog walkers and their friends.

There's more weed than ducks. Monocots outdo pennywort in the root war
an o'er east interloper, upper storey wisecracks, and I too an exotic grope.

My apps time-out on reportage of ice bombies in a hot bath. I take on the
white ute, *he's at it again*, fetching firesticks kindling this pyjama warrior.

A vegetarian trades chemical, offsets his emissions with a nitrogen fix of
green lentils. I dine on steak while a kitten plays mouse with a chicken neck.

Meditate on Death

I must depart my body to inhabit
your country—a vessel of empire
a warm occupancy gone cold. My dead
flesh is a familiar loss—a duplicitous rot
that soil-coats the memory of us.
Labour with spade and I will distend
compostable, a late gift to your country
in fistfuls of dirt. Inter my liquid mess
of bruised decay into a soft tissue slush.
Let flesh-eaters bunk in my colonies,
bacterial guests feed—a spleen, a heart,
a death march to a *microbial clock*,
lock joints and throw away sovereignty.
I am a marbled husk that clings (too tight)
a bony-corpse. A stench lures the saprobes
and the maggots raise me from the cold.
Let the colonisers settle in and the scavengers
descend before hair and bones occupy.

From 'Life after death: the science of human decomposition'
Mo Costandi, *The Guardian*, 5 May, 2015.

Testament

no fake flowers / natives please /
uncut / rooted in the ground /
endemic to this land / roll me in dirt /
bury me shallow / plant natives please /
uncut / ditch this vessel / where birds
pierce flowers / local to soil /
let maggots feed / and fungi ravage /
and life can proceed / without a trace

… ORBITING JUNK OF MISSING PERSONS.

Mise-en-Scène of Departure

I place the pieces that were left …
furniture and forms, the colour
yellow. The piano is tacet.
A final adieu on the Laminex
in pools of ice—a chicken unbroken.
The Maidenhair etiolated toward
a lamp left on, pokes tendrils
through pierced vinyl. He will walk
through that door soon, to the impress
on the pillow, the wedding gown's list
its refusal to heel. The still life
of black hairs in the drain, forensics
can attest as once resident.
The slacks on the Hills Hoist welcome
me back. False hope. Even photographs
bolt, only spit and image liminal remains.
The abandoned props could be launched
into space, orbiting junk of missing persons.
How long will he sit and look
at the vanishing point? A flyscreen unsays
snared by unclaimed endings.

THE TIMEPIECE

A clock observes a heartbeat's arrest
in each room semaphores signal
a different time, conservation cleaners
stir-up dust to maintain the complexion
of a coral posy. Youth is the benefit
of crepe kept in an attic bustling to canter
from the bit of crinoline. The caw
of crow's feet held at arm's length
her two sons wave a redundant alphabet
brought to you by the letters g r i e and f.

Ghosting

Being cat-less is showing up to Mother's Day—a bag lady whose trolley rolled under a bus en route to Hay St Mall. Kitten heels tap pavements, clip claws one paw pad at-a-time. A nasal RAT is a pregnancy test that insists, I'm still cursed. Hello Kitty waves from counter tops while fertility is a full purse reimbursed. Well-endowed steamed dumplings—swollen Demi Moore's. *Look at me, I'm cat-less*—in an empty house being pinned to the bed, a cat on my heart.

Hostile Design

Shy of the artifice of Coco Chanel
defence architecture.
Back-alley price tags   little black dress
& safe sex, I muse & photograph   a spent condom.
We commute amorphous but my resistance   fissures
a mirror shard, my chipped tooth mechanism.
Hostile design acupunctures bird soles   and metal studs
make for a   rough ride skate on concrete sliders
and I wonder why it smells of   piss when the lights
come on. I check my reflection in a   rear-view lapel
all pseudo independent,   tough edged flight. A shopfront
with six cures   for foreign sausage   the night
of broken glass   maladaptive returned servicemen
fracture inner child.

Faux Contrite

In the laundry house penitent hands
are never seen idle. A Titian Magdalene
dissembles Victorian corsets in brushstrokes
of ruining. Bare breasts cupped by hair
posturing tears on a *Savonarola*: a U-shape
fit for rounded vowels. A fine house of
apocryphal repute, his hands wring a starched
collar. A paint rub reveals a river brown,
sash windows bestir muniments of title.
Sour wine and gall in crystal. She'll crawl
the fourteen steps redressed by balustrade
to abscond from the widow's walk: *loved
and loathed.*

THE CHANGEROOM

An hydraulic arm orchestrates
a tempest
the moment I step in
the concrete monument. Some say
dig in
an homage to permanence, others say
retreat, the rise
and slap, a seawall
caulk, the claw
and carry, the scale of hubris
pitch
fluctuating to dampen the sea.
I am afoot
with no cost benefit
a mantle in the Ladies' apse
knee deep
in a dissonant cavity.
The way
some see it—
if we set a precedent
there's no looking back.
A child, a reclamation
a shell
flush to their ear
listing.

Domestic Ardour

Air pressure is my knight
pounds per inch.
The spectacle of life's de-
silvering, twilight
bunked on an antique sardine
dish. I trail flocked
wallpaper, the scale of cockatoo
tail to hold hands
with doorknobs—the relief of risk.
To press into Gyprock
encounter friction
my cornered hips inclined to niche.
I fall hard for carpet
stubble, brush knees and palms
fingers lock
in a shag pile loop. The westerly
whispers sweet-talk
as I knead flour and yeast and make
believe.

Bed Bugs Can Kill a Hotel's Reputation

there are mattresses airing on the street
for the whole world to see an ache writ
loud. the sag is a keepsake upcycled to
redistribute as carpet underlay. the husk
of our love is a doormat. an innerspring
creak is a bed-in-a-box amnesiac, draw
a line down the middle and send him in-
to the night. a kerbside mattress is a trial
of queens. stack up the capitalists' throw
downs to detect a pea.
where are the inventos of Centro Habana
who make reparations of dirty laundry?
infatuation on the left-hand side. spoon a
pillow, coo an incline for firm. the moon
wanes dissent, a futon towed three flights
pauses at each landing until he complains,
there's no spring back. a ghoul at the foot
of the bed declares, he died today. sharks
lurk, an inheritance stashed amid stitched
lining. a gibbous cyst soaks through three
towels. memory foam rebounds to forget.
fear sleep insomniac. toss and rotate each
month. all the stories in life are told, loss
disappointment, the tousle of the overlay
you kept me up all night.

Whatnot

Were ladylike letters ever penned
from the French *secrétaire*
with a masculine article? The morning
room is a sanctum of confidence
with two doors and a whatnot
upcycled from butter box and spools
that unravel. Does she indite script
and risk spectacles that don't yet exist
to be spun by an imp into golden skein?
Her mansion is earthed in fence wire
hooked rag rugs and grass tree resin.
She grows tea roses, buds, and thorns
but there are no poppies self-seeding.
They are deadheaded by walking sticks.

Gold Dot on Maroon

To play dish Jenga
with dinner plates, cups
and saucers
we console ourselves
she lays the best
table
gold dot on maroon
dishwasher safe.
To tiptoe
along gilt rim
vitrified
glaze   in a sink of Palmolive
split lip
on porcelain dentata
we let him go home
to her.
To dissent
front fists against grist
whumps
impermeable   mass-
produced
ceramic service, between
pity
and Invidia
to hand-painted china.
I buy her crockery.

How to Stay Put

The world news arrives
on my front doorstep.
It knocks like an unexpected
guest. A filmy residue
sticks on the closed door
a retracted handshake.
My body tempts as hostess
to contaminated touch.
I retreat and remove
the welcome mat. I nest
and fatten on yeasty rolls
fresh baked and remember
my mother's mothers
know how to domesticate.
You'll find it in seeds
their voice disperses
fecundity. I dig in
plant kept envelopes
of dormant hope. Chuck
pumpkin, bathe beet-tops
until they root and plant
in a sunny spot. Fend off
pests that threaten to spoil
with soap and water
and wait.

THE WAITING ROOM

In a skiff poised to ferry
with a coin donation paid-up,
I'm a bench chained to a Flooded
Gum that enthrals in wet feet.
My lap belt restraint is a wowser.
Risk averse. The egret is a witch
paddling chamber pots.
Even the colouring-in books are
too damp to kindle. Oh!
To be naked lolling in tobacco
ready to smoke! I swipe right
for an escort and make haste
to lawns of tragedy
but I'm stymied by a dupe
with his pants down
looking for a misplaced doll.

Visiting Window

I remain behind glass
in a cabinet of skin
for the in-person parade:
an aged care curio.
Loneliness is a glass cloche
your breath fogs
and petals flatten

---

just out of reach.

... YOU CAN BE ANYTHING WITH A TAN.

Outer Suburban Fog

The GPS is set on The Spray Tan Salon, where the freeway gives way to a clear-cut green demise. *The Dreamtime trail* skirts sentinel pine. A surface dune sips an absinthe haze. A church sits elevated; the cross intersects blue sky on the right side of *Marmion Ave. Troy for Lawnmowing* is nailed to a telegraph pole out-processed by *Affordable Artificial Grass* just past *The Mole Clinic.* A window frames a sister village; the dozers foreshadowing a Grass Tree fog. Pelicans' pulpit sermons *three hundred metres from the beach*; a magpie carols, *Cockleshell Place* by a *Thirsty Camel* drive-thru on a family friendly street. A poet must have been hired by *Lend Lease* and I wonder what other company wants our service? Beach huts repose for hire, undress design guidelines in lambs' wool white. They congregate for sea views on *Eden Beach* where a blonde boy holds a dead fish, the holy trinity: *sun, sea,* and *sand.* East of Eden two-by-two strips of grass for Troy to mow and elevated plots. But for now, the *mobile dog* wash parks and the spray-on-tan entrepreneur reassures, "*you can be anything with a tan*".

Italicised words are from street and business signs.

THE STRANGER

<table>
<tr><td>declarations drown</td><td>unfathomable silence</td></tr>
<tr><td>good ships pass us</td><td>by, and we pass harbouring</td></tr>
<tr><td>they</td><td>anchor at sea</td></tr>
<tr><td>untether nights</td><td>idle days on</td></tr>
<tr><td>stateless horizons</td><td></td></tr>
<tr><td>not knowing who</td><td></td></tr>
<tr><td>will claim</td><td>them.</td></tr>
<tr><td>and who will save</td><td>us.</td></tr>
<tr><td></td><td>a global sink of condemnation</td></tr>
<tr><td>while their chance sails</td><td>our pirates' pride is</td></tr>
<tr><td>reputed</td><td>lilting starboard</td></tr>
<tr><td></td><td>our namesake stains</td></tr>
<tr><td></td><td>the ledger of the deep.</td></tr>
<tr><td>can't say</td><td>we didn't know</td></tr>
<tr><td>don't need</td><td></td></tr>
<tr><td>another</td><td>irreconcilable.</td></tr>
<tr><td>stern deterrents</td><td>mock</td></tr>
<tr><td>maritime distress flags</td><td>our signal to buoy</td></tr>
<tr><td></td><td></td></tr>
<tr><td>the stranger</td><td>for</td></tr>
</table>

they are us.

Odoriferous Diorama

A plastic garlic bulb is on display in the museum as an ethnic contribution to our state. Plastic covered sofas reserved for special guests in my father's *zia's** parlour. We sit on them once upon arrival but now congregate familiar around the Formica table. The plastic cloves are indivisible now quotas, that separated north from south, tolerate warm tones. A plastic garlic, the colour of milk fat on the cappuccino strip, umbrellas waft, papery skins lift, the sea breeze ventilates alfresco dining. I should be grateful for the assimilation of the plastic artefact.

* zia is Italian for aunt.

Need Not Apply

Even as an apostate, I smart at the record
brown shoes need not apply to occupy
the establishment. Doors and hallways
are social apartheid, where the breezeway
sublimates airs. My lineage is a turncoat
betrothed in the sacristy like smells and bells
to the service door in exchange for graft.
Saturday's girl is the gig economy, black boots
ring for drones and Deliveroo on-demand.
To live in unnamed, a noun-as-verb we assert
is not lace. Doors close and jambs hinge
the landed trickle a few bob through the gaps
in the hagiography of pork barrels collected
by the unnamed need not apply. I could tear
down these columns with chaise longue inflection
flail strips off my labourer's scent to purse lips
at pool, not pull and still retain my class.

Unpick

In pieces
the cameo is levelled.
        The side view is umbral
service doors keep linen privy.
Her fingers loop around a waist
        deep in hot water
her cheekbones outgrow
the hand-me-downs:
        a two-tiered cotton-reel
stand reduced to a carnelian peach
delivering heirs.
        If you unclasp
the brooch, unpick the *chemise*, lay out
the bodice front and centre back, she'd be
        an inversion
a bust raised against *intaglio*, a miniature
scene at the throat. Their portraits are
        mistress then maid
a close-up
then a long shot.

Christmas Haikus

Nuytsia floribunda is lit
the carpark is full

—

suburban reindeers compete
unpaid bills

—

the tree stays boxed
empty nesters

—

cat vomits prawn head
a family gathers

Class Consciousness

On my first day as writer in residence
I startle the cleaner
and when the power
stops working, my ineptitude with power
means the handyman
drops by to sort out my power
needs. I theorise
that it might be the cleaner's
vacuum and my power
sources tripping. *You mean, J.?*
he corrects me.
Yes, like my mother
who was cleaner, then barmaid, then bed
and breakfast proprietor.
The handyman logically deducts the power
board is faulty. He crawls
under the table to plug my devices
directly into the power
point and asks, *Are you okay with this?*
Of course, confused he thinks, I can't crawl.
I sit to rewrite the working class
into history and ask the volunteers
if anyone knows the servants' names beyond cook and
coachman? Loyalty portraits hang mid-stair
as I write words into their mouths.
They look bemused
with the extension of their work-in-hand
but they politely indulge me.

Tourist Trade

A police van draws a line
outside The Visitor's Centre. The Bottle O
is a sobriety test, where my husband and I spar
over which flavour beer to purchase.
I lie low in the shade
of a wide-brimmed hat, while he brokers
with a merchant over a boab nut
who looks right under
at garish coloured beads.
Men shuck oysters, imports
from Coffin Bay, spit out
a two-thousand-year-old pearl. We visit
'The Lookout', it is number two 'To Do'
in the tourist brochure. A red carpet
tongue, we sip views. The laser cut
shadows illuminate tidal flats.
There! I point
navigate down pindan dirt. People picnic
trade a wave, toast a vessel.
I beg
to go
when we get
bogged.
I close the windows while he pushes.
In an Art gallery
mirror to my hat, storm shutters shade and hide
heritage listing. I walk the gaps
in the planks. The wind tunnel is blocked.

On a wall, a teardrop suspends, incised rouge
of ceremony
of manhood
of trade
it is steam and close.
We swill beer behind a picket fence,
sea-eagles circle. We booze in the haze
a half kilo of prawns—not having oysters.

Suffragette Bluebells

He was determined we would carry equal amounts. We packed to sustain a night on the Bibbulmun Track. My backpack was a cheap Big W sack. No support and sagging way behind, so as I walked, I held it aloft to give my aching lumbar some respite. We carried our own water in, an extra litre, just in case. The dusty ground moved beneath me, startling as the water jostled to my gait—a walking waterbed in tow. I joined him in the wonder that was mainly on the ground, as little trips sprang forth. Jutting rocks and roots defied the tramping of the snake signed fork. The sun was high and unrepentantly drained me, as the backpack, despite the regular gulping seemed to get leaden upon my back. He whistled while he walked ahead and often out of sight. I stumbled here and there and focused less. The kilometres accrued but destination never seemed to find me. My hands now moved beneath the sack, and fists held tight pressed close against my back to ease the thudding pain. He whistled and was out of sight, but I kept my pride in check, not wanting him to think, I couldn't handle it. At last, I bowed down to respite, and sat, then lay upon my back, back sack still on, and laying in that trampled dirt. I didn't care that he was gone. I would rest and wait. I felt a calm surrender that I hadn't felt throughout the year that was the school year marathon that every year swamps and punishes. A conveyer belt of clouds moved by, and I plunged right into childhood, no daisy chains, but there aground, suffragette bluebells. I limply called his name but knew he wouldn't hear, for he was marching way ahead in whistling rapture. I held him back this time of year, but he bravely kept me going, each term three as I sunk stubbornly determined to surrender. But something, someone always stopped me.

And there it was. It landed. Without sound or fanfare. A robin. It was red. And rotated to-and-fro so close I felt it knew but was not afraid of me.

THE CRYSTAL PALACE ON HAY ST. MALL

A contraction of foot traffic signals
the slow collapse of an empire
off-trend like Victoria's bust in a
mink stole down a Milan runway.
The window display is a *bon marché*,
a mannequin head in sand. Modern
Spartacus wears acid wash but can't
pay back a credit card debt on the
gig economy. But you look a million
dollars on a dollar a day while muzak
wafts, Ariana Grande's base notes of
marshmallow—eau de break through …

Not-For-Profit

The aerial view is flat
and dry, sparse and utilitarian.
Grid patterns map spoils
of corrupt zeal. We fly-in
with bones, morality with-
drawn from an ATM.
He arrives hungry. Hunger
hangs-on the moment
we land, soliciting gifts
we give back. His hole
is insatiable. He eats pre-dinner
then cleans up the leftovers.
We fight over needs that might
not be met, his hunger—
my need to flee this mission
called team. We consume
fair. Freedom that money affords
choice. Friends like us spend-up
big on street kids' brownies
spring rolls dipped in chilli
sauce and prawn crackers washed
down with a pineapple daquiri.
The more we eat, the more charity
provides relief.

A MAGIC TRICK TO SLIP THROUGH ...

Property Rights

A *femme covert* is a roof overhead
slippers in the doll's house to roleplay
a contract to wedlock. Her bequest
is Shetland lace held by a napkin ring
as protection loophole. *Hush-hush*
she needles open space with bobbin yarn
a magic trick to slip through and prate
her own name.

THE MUSE AS ARTIST

for Jeanne Héburtene

I am all hair.
A maiden's hair frames eyes of blue.
You dip me in oil. A neck.   A wine-soaked scarf.
I am the verse to your brush   that breathes amphoric
along my thighs.   A gilded arrow pierces a destitute cave.
I look up from blue   as you scatter doves that plump
on seed.   My crown is myrtle free, yet still, I swell.
I am   all hair. Two rose coils adorn   the muse.
I braid the strands of moonlight.   The artist. On hold
while I sit still.   I am all hair and I hold nothing back.
I brood under your wing.   They sit. We paint.
You paint the caves that dwell.   I paint
the cave dwellings.   My eyes untruss the future.
Window frames to blue.   I watch your husk
in bottles at my feet   where doves once fattened.
I smell death.   It clings and I hold on
devoted to your tragic fate.   The muse that leaps
when arrows turn to lead.   Another bastard
I cannot bear.

Travelling Towards Light

after 'Diving into the Wreck' *by Adrienne Rich*

Begin reading the book of capes
and burden the backpack
and wade new boots to walk in
suit up
the zip-up khaki pants
the wicking beige shirt
the wide and toggled hat.
Choose to spend this
sun-drenched summer not
lazing indefinitely
atop a sun-screened hazed towel
but between lights.

There is a sand dune.
The sand dune is arduous
insidiously softening
sinks in deep each foot each time.
Grow to accept it's
you who have to traverse it.
Anyways
it is a path of barren surprise
a cross trainer to high.

Lumber up.
Foot after sinking foot
the sand infiltrates boots
the heels scrape
the socks squeak
of mewling calves.
Lumber up.
A shoelace unravels you.
Drag like a flailing mule up the dune
and no porter will
save you when the summit
will appear.

Initially, the sand is coarse and then
it is sunlit and then quartz and then
blank and you are blanking out and yet
your will is tenacious
it fills your marrow with fire
the sand is a douser of fire
the sand is not fanned air.
You must keep on scaling
to sink your feet in surrender
in the scattered prints.

And now: your mind journeys
away from ancient paths who wear
anointed feet
caressing their treaded boots
beside the eroding coast
and besides
you think radically up here.

Choose to hike between the lights.
The paths are mortal.
The paths are guide.
Come to see the fortitude you have
and the animal that inhabits.
Stroke the flame of your pride
gingerly, you balance the rise
of aspiring to something
more than creaky knees.

The prize you walk for:
the light and not the lighthouse
the path itself and not the destined
the bronzed face always striving
forward the lamp
the avoidance of wrecks slain
smashed by rocks and reefs of these converging seas
the grains of sands last
former wrecks strewn
amongst the Indian and Southern breaks.

This is Wardandi land.
And you are here, the gullible pilgrim
steams sweat, the pilgrim with her fragile past.
You plod hastily
near the light
you almost race towards.
Be house: be light

whose blinkered eye nought sleeps sound
whose tower bears the lash of wind
whose sand flogs abrasive scars
scales white painted flanks
welts painted over again.
You are the vandal of empires
that still spoil to traverse
the convergence of two seas
the wind stoked water course.

You are house. You are light. Reach
by folly or virility
the one who crosses the dune
each foot in time
porting a map, a sandwich
the guidebook
in which
your footprints disappear.

Carrion Flower

I withdraw the blood money from your fatality
and chew betel nut to get high.
    Hot *ringgit* profits
where swiftlets coalesce
and a noose that hangs at Madai Cave corrupts
when pulled.
    Metal against rock echolocates off cave walls
    to scrape and sell on to the affluents'
penchant for spit.
I travel light
    with a bottle of Scotch, a cheesecloth frock
    like your returned wallet, a helmet damned.
The mosquito repellent can't conceal
a gangrenous leg
chase after me down jungle tracks.
I parasitise—a terrestrial leech,
toast Nepenthe's sorrow,
    to the blood rust on your last five.
    The bloom—a Rafflesia on the eighth day,
purplish around the lip.
    Your fetid exhalation
    where carrion flies soar.

THE BREAKDOWN

My first thought is pass by and like the car before me, I keep wheels in motion hesitant to stop. For all I know her collapse is impulse amassed, but I can't unsee her absurd flight. An émigré on the traffic island: sand to berth idle from the going to

and coming back. A police van condemns another breakdown. I cede my keys, beachcomb for a wounded fowl, there for the enchain, and leap—a piebald plume on the wing of an air foil.

THE RULES OF ASYLUM

after See What You Made Me Do *by Jess Hill*

She can get help, but the rules are, you must ask first and never go back. Should I tell that woman about the restroom that isn't signposted? The security camera won't follow her home. And then I see the no frills, female ablutions secreted on the underground floor of the men's clothing department, where an unlikely woman walks out empowered by Dior classic lips. I look up at the CCTV surveillance as I'm led down a merchandiser's path. She is trailing him three steps down the escalator, and I can't help but speculate what retribution will be dealt. I unclench my fist and remind myself that this is not my dispute. A woman hollers and we all gawp. A security guard hovers, but is immobilised by the invisible line of not my job. And we all know the rules. Women go shopping with children. That's why the parent's room is adjacent to women's fashion on the first floor. But then I reflect, he won't let her go out alone with a credit card and his two kids. As the domestic scene unfolds, the French perfume wears off from the sensory experience on the ground floor, where women are on top.

Wet Breath

Rice flags wave me down. Blue lips
in a waterlogged *padi* field. *Vá xe*:
a piston in a cylinder pumping air.
The bent valve expires a chronic
cough to spill and rake over a road
to dry out the belaboured alveoli.
A buffalo drawn through the nose
to stomp sediment. Yoked shoulders
shudder—a spirometer's test.
When the crop fails cough up
a water shrimp, one basket has room
for a heart, a fish palpitates.
Remove the dust cap to inflate
a bamboo pole across an iron horse
to redistribute the weight.
A diaphragm contracts and fills
a leaky tyre. I wash my pyjamas out
each night, wear them wet to dry off
on the heat of my skin.
Two hundred kilos fan a *xe thô sơ*
belaboured beasts draw back
while I cough-up a clam
sinking in wet rice, my forehead
spattered in silt.

vá xe bike pump service
xe thô sơ modified bike

THE AGE OF RESISTANCE

When did I loosen my grip
on decisions? I resist
flesh poverty, reapply
brick-red with a compact
and lift weights. I flex
at sedentary tropes to bow
down, press shoulders
to palms and shrug off bed-rest.
A barbell composes a protest
song hummed to squats between
reps, the right to bear steel.
I choose sovereignty and outsource
dependence. I balance, not falter
and smash the frailty premise.

En Route

'There's just that feeling that this isn't a proper life, and so there is that feeling that the quicker it's all over, the better it is for everybody'
—Ms Merle Mitchell AM

A single suitcase. What will ~~*you*~~ *I* pack?
~~*Your*~~ *My* home? A 2x1, brick & tile,
boutique villa ~~*I've*~~ *you've* since spent.
Nobody wants to hear ~~*your*~~ *my* flesh
groan. ~~*You*~~ *I* will not burden ~~*me*~~ *you*
with keepsakes destined for the charity
box. ~~*You*~~ *I* can't strip away wallpaper,
the mural is dry paint, a memory stick
is a placeable face, the music on shuffle
like contact ~~*I*~~ *you* divvy between visiting
hours. Perhaps ~~*You'll*~~ *I'll* leave the suitcase
empty and when ~~*you*~~ *I* find ~~*yourself*~~ *myself*
a routine round, ~~*You'll*~~ *I'll* pocket nosegays
from the garden ~~*I*~~ *you* dug and climb in.

Ms Merle Mitchell AM quoted from the Royal Commission into Aged Care Quality and Safety, 2018

Epilogue: Poetics of Disturbia

I try to protect my mentor, L., and apologise for the dark. She tells me that 'art should go to difficult places.' We are locked down in masked isolation, so communication becomes virtually intimate. Online, sunsets bleed recurrently in a speculative dimension, while a bushfire burns on the ground. It is a familiar crisis. Friends share posts of cremains cloaking their suburbs like it's extraordinary. I run to be free of the gag, and after thirty-eight years of waking up to the smell of smoke-filled hair, I write the next edit.

Lucy tells me that poems are like 'dipping pools'. I ascertain the exact depth of dread and synchronise with ghosts in tandem laps on suburban streets. It is difficult to do so. When I begin to flounder, she seems to know the precise moment to intervene. I study the mechanics of treading water, and sink alongside keystones and unbearable weights.

I sit on the bottom. With each new rewrite, my jaw clamps shut. I hold my breath to interrogate the history of gun laws, only to find cold facts and statistics. I read tabloid stories that could have been about us: a potential headline shot from a family album. I present Lucy with an iceberg. It's all I can write. She talks of 'condensed drama in relation to other work,' and subsequently I begin to look beyond vignettes and see a prospective manuscript.

I'm on retreat. My inner world is awash and escape to Katharine's Place is timely. I pack an esky with provisions and take a pile of books. Lucy says, 'read what you're drawn to.' I read Randolph Stow's poems and climate change warnings. I take copious notes about obscure female artists. I switch off my phone but it's hard to resist. When I settle for mute, a woman on Marketplace pesters me about a red cocktail dress. I resolve to write about checking into a motel room with a *nom de plume* and stubbornly ignore her. Yet, when I escape the city for the hills, I find myself in-between departure and arrivals. Some details I include and some I leave out, like the exact number of shards, and how the Holden was reported stolen. I draw from art installations to glean the colour of fright and write a gothic Australian dream.

I wake to the smell of toast in my hair. It's 3am and I wonder if this is Katharine's ghost? Between her fireplace and my cottage is a chilling reminder: the prickly pear's pulped flesh with barbs of defence scores a blue sky. I walk laps of the neighbourhood and come across hope sown through the herb garden, nestled between the tomes of a street library, and etched in an R U OK tree. But there are gargoyles too, and a Doric column.

I speak of the dark as witness. Because it happens to us, to families in suburbs, around the Laminex.

Attributions to the following authors and their work:

'Dishonour' contains lines from: 'The Pleasures of the Damned' by Charles Bukowski; *Tender is the Night* by F. Scott Fitzgerald; *On the Road* by Jack Kerouac; and *A Woman Like Her* by Sanam Maher.

How to Order Eggs Sunny Side Up
by Lisa Collyer

I would like to acknowledge and pay respect to the Whadjuk people of the Noongar nation and elders past, present and emerging.

How to Order Eggs Sunny Side Up (as a preliminary manuscript) was shortlisted for The Dorothy Hewett Award, 2022.

Acknowledgement is made to the following publications in which some of these poems first appeared: *Science Write Now*, 2023; *Australian Poetry Anthology*, Australian Poetry, 2022; *Cordite Poetry Review*, 2021, 2022; *Creatrix no. 49, 50, 51*, Poets Inc, 2020; *fourW thirty-one New Writing*, 2021; *Letters to our Home*, Follow that cat, 2020; *Meniscus Literary Journal,* 2022; *Not Very Quiet Journal,* 2021; *Poetry d'Amour*, Poets Inc, 2020; *Rabbit nonfiction journal*, Rabbit Poetry, 2021, 2022; *Recoil 12*, Mulla Mulla Press, 2021; *Social Alternatives vol. 40, no.3*, Poetry to the Rescue, 2021; *The Saltbush Review Issue 3,* 2023; *The Underground Writers Issue 32,* 2020; *Westerly Magazine 66.2*, UWA Publishing, 2021; *Westerly Magazine online,* UWA Publishing, 2021*; Wrong Way Go Back: vol. 19*, Pure Slush, 2020.

With thanks to Westerly Magazine Writers' Development Program, Lucy Dougan, The National Trust of W.A., The Four Centres' Emerging Writers' Program, WA Poets Inc., and Katharine Susannah Prichard Writers' Centre.

First published 2023

POETRY

ISBN: 978-0-6456337-6-4

BOOK, TYPESETTING, AND LOGO DESIGN
Mountains Brown Press

PUBLISHER
Life Before Man

Gazebo Books
PO Box 375
Summer Hill
New South Wales 2130
Australia

gazebobooks.com.au

This book was made possible thanks to Anthony Mark Day

COVER IMAGE: *Shed*, 2023, oil on linen, 26 x 20.5 cm, © Phil Day

www.ingramcontent.com/pod-product-compliance
Lightning Source LLC
LaVergne TN
LVHW050959080826
845145LV00009B/2360

* 9 7 8 0 6 4 5 6 3 3 7 6 4 *